# The Real Book Multi-Tracks Vol. 4

**For C, B♭, E♭ & Bass Clef Instruments**

# CHARLIE PARKER

## Play-Along

To access online content visit:
**www.halleonard.com/mylibrary**

**Enter Code**
**6432-1321-1541-5382**

ISBN 978-1-4950-7509-4

**HAL•LEONARD®**

7777 W. BLUEMOUND RD. P.O. BOX 13819 MILWAUKEE, WI 53213

For more information on the Real Book series, including community forums, please visit
**www.OfficialRealBook.com**

Visit Hal Leonard Online at
**www.halleonard.com**

# Contents

# ANTHROPOLOGY

— CHARLIE PARKER/DIZZY GILLESPIE

**C VERSION**

(FAST SWING)

*OPTIONAL

**SOLO CHANGES

FINE

# Blues for Alice

- Charlie Parker

# CONFIRMATION

— CHARLIE PARKER

C VERSION

LAST X, ⌣

# Donna Lee

— Charlie Parker

C VERSION

FINE

# K.C. BLUES

— CHARLIE PARKER

C VERSION

AFTER SOLOS, D.S. AL ⨁
(PLAY PICKUP)

# Moose The Mooche

- Charlie Parker

C VERSION

(FAST SWING)

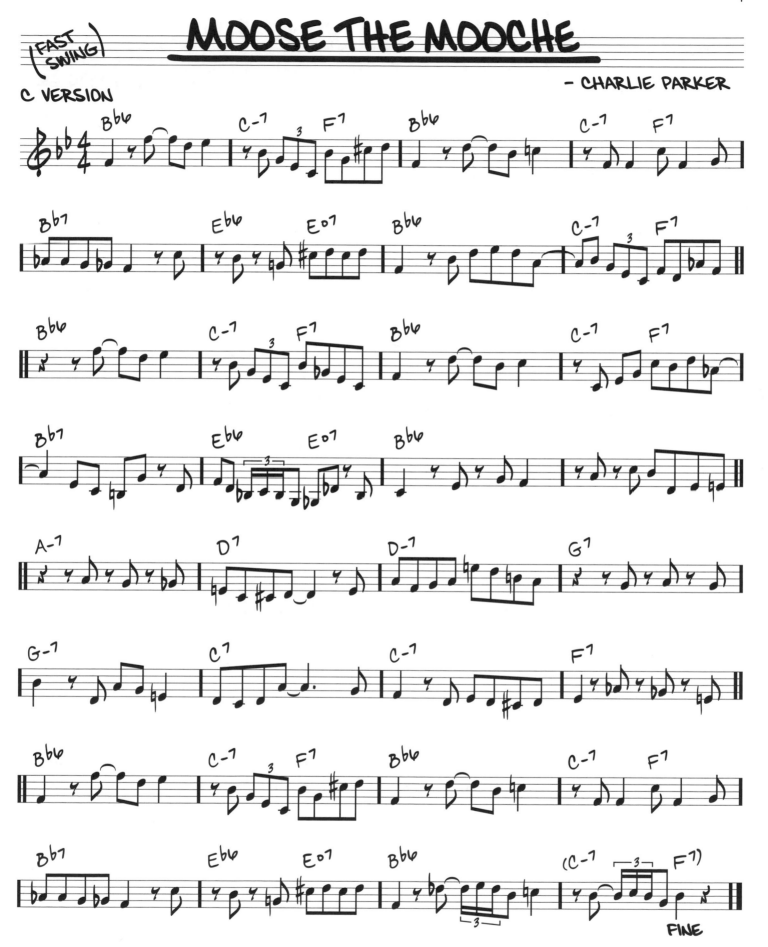

FINE

# My Little Suede Shoes

— CHARLIE PARKER

C VERSION

FINE

# ORNITHOLOGY

– CHARLIE PARKER/BENNIE HARRIS

# SCRAPPLE FROM THE APPLE

- CHARLIE PARKER

# Yardbird Suite

— CHARLIE PARKER

C Version

AFTER SOLOS, D.C. AL ✛
(TAKE REPEAT)

# ANTHROPOLOGY

— CHARLIE PARKER/DIZZY GILLESPIE

# BLUES FOR ALICE

– CHARLIE PARKER

# CONFIRMATION

– CHARLIE PARKER

(FAST SWING)

B♭ VERSION

# Donna Lee

– CHARLIE PARKER

**B♭ Version**

FINE

# K.C. BLUES

– CHARLIE PARKER

# Moose The Mooche

— Charlie Parker

(FAST SWING)

Bb VERSION

# MY LITTLE SUEDE SHOES

— CHARLIE PARKER

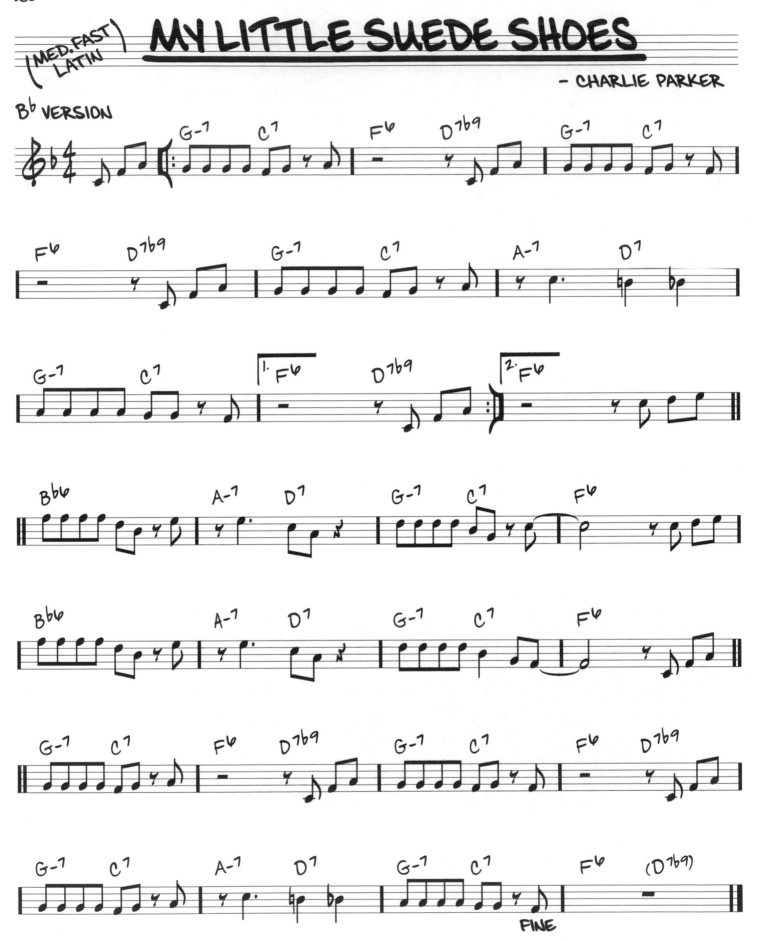

# ORNITHOLOGY

— CHARLIE PARKER / BENNIE HARRIS

# SCRAPPLE FROM THE APPLE

*(FAST SWING)*

– CHARLIE PARKER

**B♭ VERSION**

FINE

# Yardbird Suite

— CHARLIE PARKER

AFTER SOLOS, D.C. AL ⊕
(TAKE REPEAT)

# Anthropology

— Charlie Parker / Dizzy Gillespie

E♭ Version

(FAST SWING)

**OPTIONAL

**SOLO CHANGES

FINE

# Blues For Alice

– CHARLIE PARKER

# CONFIRMATION

— CHARLIE PARKER

# Donna Lee

Eb Version

— Charlie Parker

# K.C. Blues

— CHARLIE PARKER

AFTER SOLOS, D.S. AL ⊕
(PLAY PICKUP)

# Moose The Mooche

— Charlie Parker

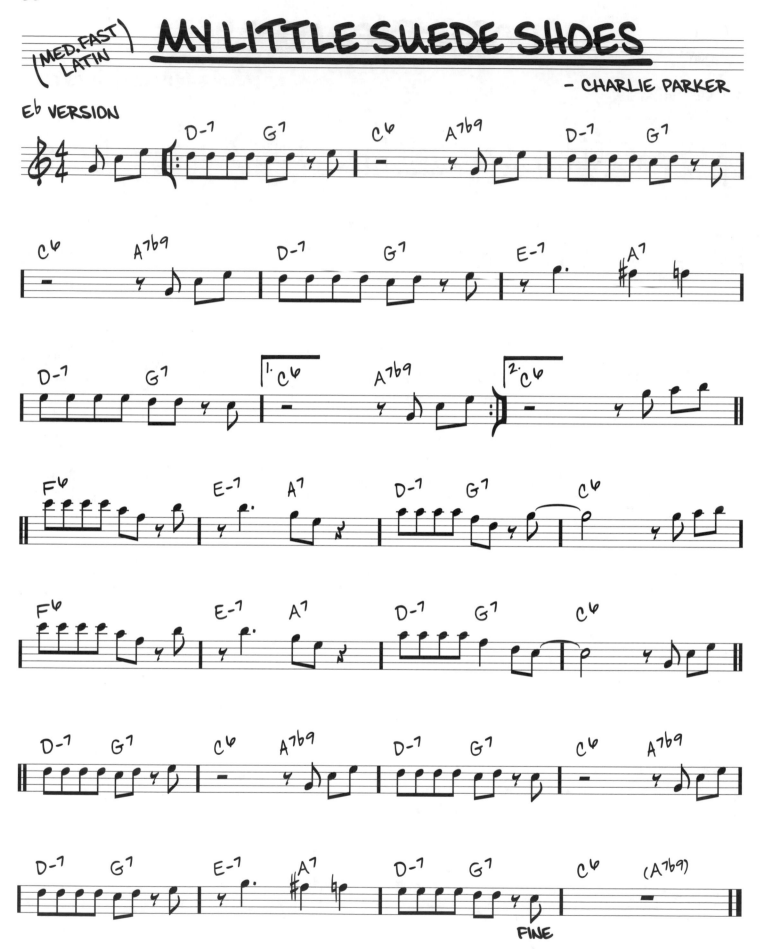

# ORNITHOLOGY

– CHARLIE PARKER/BENNIE HARRIS

Eb VERSION

# SCRAPPLE FROM THE APPLE

– CHARLIE PARKER

# Yardbird Suite

— Charlie Parker

Eb Version

AFTER SOLOS, D.C. AL ⊕
(TAKE REPEAT)

# ANTHROPOLOGY

- Charlie Parker / Dizzy Gillespie

C BASS VERSION

(FAST SWING)

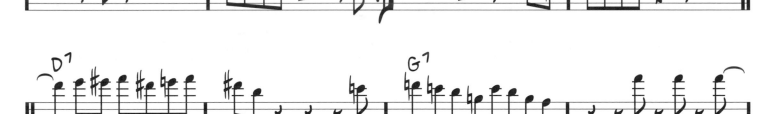

**SOLO CHANGES

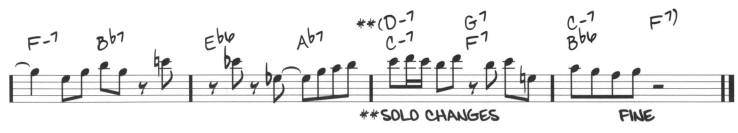

FINE

# Blues For Alice

— CHARLIE PARKER

# Confirmation

— CHARLIE PARKER

C BASS VERSION

(FAST SWING)

# Donna Lee

C BASS VERSION

— CHARLIE PARKER

FINE

# K.C. BLUES

— CHARLIE PARKER

C BASS VERSION

AFTER SOLOS, D.S. AL ⊕
(PLAY PICKUP)

# Moose The Mooche

(FAST SWING)

C BASS VERSION

– CHARLIE PARKER

FINE

# My Little Suede Shoes

— CHARLIE PARKER

C BASS VERSION

# ORNITHOLOGY

— CHARLIE PARKER/BENNIE HARRIS

C BASS VERSION

# SCRAPPLE FROM THE APPLE

– CHARLIE PARKER

(FAST SWING)

C BASS VERSION

# Yardbird Suite

— CHARLIE PARKER

C BASS VERSION

AFTER SOLOS, D.C. AL ⊕
(TAKE REPEAT)

# THE REAL BOOK MULTI-TRACKS

## 1. MAIDEN VOYAGE PLAY-ALONG
Autumn Leaves • Blue Bossa • Doxy • Footprints • Maiden Voyage • Now's the Time • On Green Dolphin Street • Satin Doll • Summertime • Tune Up.
00196616  Book with Online Media .................................................. $17.99

## 2. MILES DAVIS PLAY-ALONG
Blue in Green • Boplicity (Be Bop Lives) • Four • Freddie Freeloader • Milestones • Nardis • Seven Steps to Heaven • So What • Solar • Walkin'.
00196798  Book with Online Media ................................................. $17.99

## 3. ALL BLUES PLAY-ALONG
All Blues • Back at the Chicken Shack • Billie's Bounce (Bill's Bounce) • Birk's Works • Blues by Five • C-Jam Blues • Mr. P.C. • One for Daddy-O • Reunion Blues • Turnaround.
00196692  Book with Online Media ................................................. $17.99

## 4. CHARLIE PARKER PLAY-ALONG
Anthropology • Blues for Alice • Confirmation • Donna Lee • K.C. Blues • Moose the Mooche • My Little Suede Shoes • Ornithology • Scrapple from the Apple • Yardbird Suite.
00196799  Book with Online Media ................................................. $17.99

## 5. JAZZ FUNK PLAY-ALONG
Alligator Bogaloo • The Chicken • Cissy Strut • Cold Duck Time • Comin' Home Baby • Mercy, Mercy, Mercy • Put It Where You Want It • Sidewinder • Tom Cat • Watermelon Man.
00196728  Book with Online Media ....................... $17.99

THE REAL BOOK MULTI-TRACKS Play-Along

# The Best-Selling Jazz Book of All Time Is Now Legal!

The Real Books are the most popular jazz books of all time. Since the 1970s, musicians have trusted these volumes to get them through every gig, night after night. The problem is that the books were illegally produced and distributed, without any regard to copyright law, or royalties paid to the composers who created these musical masterpieces.

Hal Leonard is very proud to present the first legitimate and legal editions of these books ever produced. You won't even notice the difference, other than all the notorious errors being fixed: the covers and typeface look the same, the song lists are nearly identical, and the price for our edition is even cheaper than the originals!

Every conscientious musician will appreciate that these books are now produced accurately and ethically, benefitting the songwriters that we owe for some of the greatest tunes of all time!

## VOLUME 1
| | | |
|---|---|---|
| 00240221 | C Edition | $39.99 |
| 00240224 | B♭ Edition | $39.99 |
| 00240225 | E♭ Edition | $39.99 |
| 00240226 | Bass Clef Edition | $39.99 |
| 00240292 | C Edition 6 x 9 | $35.00 |
| 00240339 | B♭ Edition 6 x 9 | $35.00 |
| 00147792 | Bass Clef Edition 6 x 9 | $35.00 |
| 00451087 | C Edition on CD-ROM | $29.99 |
| 00240302 | A-D CD Backing Tracks | $24.99 |
| 00240303 | E-J CD Backing Tracks | $24.95 |
| 00240305 | S-Z CD Backing Tracks | $24.99 |
| 00110604 | Book/USB Flash Drive Backing Tracks Pack | $79.99 |
| 00110599 | USB Flash Drive Only | $50.00 |

## VOLUME 2
| | | |
|---|---|---|
| 00240222 | C Edition | $39.99 |
| 00240227 | B♭ Edition | $39.99 |
| 00240228 | E♭ Edition | $39.99 |
| 00240229 | Bass Clef Edition | $39.99 |
| 00240293 | C Edition 6 x 9 | $35.00 |
| 00125900 | B♭ Edition 6 x 9 | $35.00 |
| 00451088 | C Edition on CD-ROM | $30.99 |
| 00240351 | A-D CD Backing Tracks | $24.99 |
| 00240352 | E-I CD Backing Tracks | $24.99 |
| 00240353 | J-R CD Backing Tracks | $24.99 |
| 00240354 | S-Z CD Backing Tracks | $24.99 |

## VOLUME 3
| | | |
|---|---|---|
| 00240233 | C Edition | $39.99 |
| 00240284 | B♭ Edition | $39.99 |
| 00240285 | E♭ Edition | $39.99 |
| 00240286 | Bass Clef Edition | $39.99 |
| 00240338 | C Edition 6 x 9 | $35.00 |
| 00451089 | C Edition on CD-ROM | $29.99 |

## VOLUME 4
| | | |
|---|---|---|
| 00240296 | C Edition | $39.99 |
| 00103348 | B♭ Edition | $39.99 |
| 00103349 | E♭ Edition | $39.99 |
| 00103350 | Bass Clef Edition | $39.99 |

## VOLUME 5
| | | |
|---|---|---|
| 00240349 | C Edition | $39.99 |

## VOLUME 6
| | | |
|---|---|---|
| 00240534 | C Edition | $39.99 |

### Also available:
| | | |
|---|---|---|
| 00240264 | The Real Blues Book | $34.99 |
| 00310910 | The Real Bluegrass Book | $29.99 |
| 00240440 | The Trane Book | $22.99 |
| 00125426 | The Real Country Book | $39.99 |
| 00240137 | Miles Davis Real Book | $19.95 |
| 00240355 | The Real Dixieland Book C Edition | $29.99 |
| 00122335 | The Real Dixieland Book B♭ Edition | $29.99 |
| 00240235 | The Duke Ellington Real Book | $19.99 |
| 00240268 | The Real Jazz Solos Book | $30.00 |
| 00240348 | The Real Latin Book C Edition | $37.50 |
| 00127107 | The Real Latin Book B♭ Edition | $35.00 |
| 00240358 | The Charlie Parker Real Book | $19.99 |
| 00240331 | The Bud Powell Real Book | $19.99 |
| 00240437 | The Real R&B Book | $39.99 |
| 00240313 | The Real Rock Book | $35.00 |
| 00240323 | The Real Rock Book – Vol. 2 | $35.00 |
| 00240359 | The Real Tab Book | $32.50 |
| 00240317 | The Real Worship Book | $29.99 |

### THE REAL CHRISTMAS BOOK
| | | |
|---|---|---|
| 00240306 | C Edition | $32.50 |
| 00240345 | B♭ Edition | $32.50 |
| 00240346 | E♭ Edition | $32.50 |
| 00240347 | Bass Clef Edition | $32.50 |
| 00240431 | A-G CD Backing Tracks | $24.99 |
| 00240432 | H-M CD Backing Tracks | $24.99 |
| 00240433 | N-Y CD Backing Tracks | $24.99 |

### THE REAL VOCAL BOOK
| | | |
|---|---|---|
| 00240230 | Volume 1 High Voice | $35.00 |
| 00240307 | Volume 1 Low Voice | $35.00 |
| 00240231 | Volume 2 High Voice | $35.00 |
| 00240308 | Volume 2 Low Voice | $35.00 |
| 00240391 | Volume 3 High Voice | $35.00 |
| 00240392 | Volume 3 Low Voice | $35.00 |
| 00118318 | Volume 4 High Voice | $35.00 |
| 00118319 | Volume 4 Low Voice | $35.00 |

### THE REAL BOOK – STAFF PAPER
| | |
|---|---|
| 00240327 | $10.99 |

### HOW TO PLAY FROM A REAL BOOK
*by Robert Rawlins*
| | |
|---|---|
| 00312097 | $17.50 |

### THE REAL BOOK – ENHANCED CHORDS
*arranged by David Hazeltine*
| | |
|---|---|
| 00151290 | $29.99 |

**Complete song lists online at www.halleonard.com**
*Prices, content, and availability subject to change without notice.*

7777 W. BLUEMOUND RD. P.O. BOX 13819 MILWAUKEE, WI 53213

1116

# Presenting the Hal Leonard JAZZ PLAY-ALONG® SERIES

For use with all B-flat, E-flat, Bass Clef and C instruments, the Jazz Play-Along® Series is the ultimate learning tool for all jazz musicians. With musician-friendly lead sheets, melody cues, and other split-track audio choices included, these first-of-a-kind packages help you master improvisation while playing some of the greatest tunes of all time. FOR STUDY, each tune includes a split track with: melody cue with proper style and inflection • professional rhythm tracks • choruses for soloing • removable bass part • removable piano part. FOR PERFORMANCE, each tune also has: an additional full stereo accompaniment track (no melody) • additional choruses for soloing.

*These do not include split tracks.

# Jazz Instruction & Improvisation

## BOOKS FOR ALL INSTRUMENTS FROM HAL LEONARD

### AN APPROACH TO JAZZ IMPROVISATION
*by Dave Pozzi*
*Musicians Institute Press*
Explore the styles of Charlie Parker, Sonny Rollins, Bud Powell and others with this comprehensive guide to jazz improvisation. Covers: scale choices • chord analysis • phrasing • melodies • harmonic progressions • more.
00695135  Book/CD Pack..........................$17.95

### THE ART OF MODULATING
FOR PIANISTS AND JAZZ MUSICIANS
*by Carlos Salzedo &*
*Lucile Lawrence*
*Schirmer*
*The Art of Modulating* is a treatise originally intended for the harp, but this edition has been edited for use by intermediate keyboardists and other musicians who have an understanding of basic music theory. In its pages you will find: table of intervals; modulation rules; modulation formulas; examples of modulation; extensions and cadences; ten fragments of dances; five characteristic pieces; and more.
50490581  ...............................................$19.99

### BUILDING A JAZZ VOCABULARY
*By Mike Steinel*
A valuable resource for learning the basics of jazz from Mike Steinel of the University of North Texas. It covers: the basics of jazz • how to build effective solos • a comprehensive practice routine • and a jazz vocabulary of the masters.
00849911  ...............................................$19.95

### THE CYCLE OF FIFTHS
*by Emile and Laura De Cosmo*
This essential instruction book provides more than 450 exercises, including hundreds of melodic and rhythmic ideas. The book is designed to help improvisors master the cycle of fifths, one of the primary progressions in music. Guaranteed to refine technique, enhance improvisational fluency, and improve sight-reading!
00311114  ...............................................$16.99

### THE DIATONIC CYCLE
*by Emile and Laura De Cosmo*
Renowned jazz educators Emile and Laura De Cosmo provide more than 300 exercises to help improvisors tackle one of music's most common progressions: the diatonic cycle. This book is guaranteed to refine technique, enhance improvisational fluency, and improve sight-reading!
00311115  ...............................................$16.95

### EAR TRAINING
*by Keith Wyatt,*
*Carl Schroeder and Joe Elliott*
*Musicians Institute Press*
Covers: basic pitch matching • singing major and minor scales • identifying intervals • transcribing melodies and rhythm • identifying chords and progressions • seventh chords and the blues • modal interchange, chromaticism, modulation • and more.
00695198  Book/Online Audio ..............................$24.99

### EXERCISES AND ETUDES FOR THE JAZZ INSTRUMENTALIST
*by J.J. Johnson*
Designed as study material and playable by any instrument, these pieces run the gamut of the jazz experience, featuring common and uncommon time signatures and keys, and styles from ballads to funk. They are progressively graded so that both beginners and professionals will be challenged by the demands of this wonderful music.
00842018  Bass Clef Edition ...................................$17.99
00842042  Treble Clef Edition ...............................$16.95

### JAZZOLOGY
THE ENCYCLOPEDIA OF JAZZ THEORY FOR ALL MUSICIANS
*by Robert Rawlins and*
*Nor Eddine Bahha*
This comprehensive resource covers a variety of jazz topics, for beginners and pros of any instrument. The book serves as an encyclopedia for reference, a thorough methodology for the student, and a workbook for the classroom.
00311167  ........................................................$19.99

### JAZZ THEORY RESOURCES
*by Bert Ligon*
*Houston Publishing, Inc.*
This is a jazz theory text in two volumes. **Volume 1 includes**: review of basic theory • rhythm in jazz performance • triadic generalization • diatonic harmonic progressions and analysis • substitutions and turnarounds • and more. **Volume 2 includes**: modes and modal frameworks • quartal harmony • extended tertian structures and triadic superimposition • pentatonic applications • coloring "outside" the lines and beyond • and more.
00030458  Volume 1 .............................................$39.95
00030459  Volume 2 .............................................$29.95

### JOY OF IMPROV
*by Dave Frank*
*and John Amaral*
This book/audio course on improvisation for all instruments and all styles will help players develop monster musical skills! Book One imparts a solid basis in technique, rhythm, chord theory, ear training and improv concepts. **Book Two** explores more advanced chord voicings, chord arranging techniques and more challenging blues and melodic lines. The audio can be used as a listening and play-along tool.
00220005  Book 1 – Book/CD Pack......................$27.99
00220006  Book 2 – Book/Online Audio..............$26.99

### THE PATH TO JAZZ IMPROVISATION
*by Emile and Laura De Cosmo*
This fascinating jazz instruction book offers an innovative, scholarly approach to the art of improvisation. It includes in-depth analysis and lessons about: cycle of fifths • diatonic cycle • overtone series • pentatonic scale • harmonic and melodic minor scale • polytonal order of keys • blues and bebop scales • modes • and more.
00310904  ...............................................$14.99

### THE SOURCE
THE DICTIONARY OF CONTEMPORARY AND TRADITIONAL SCALES
*by Steve Barta*
This book serves as an informative guide for people who are looking for good, solid information regarding scales, chords, and how they work together. It provides right and left hand fingerings for scales, chords, and complete inversions. Includes over 20 different scales, each written in all 12 keys.
00240885  ...............................................$19.99

### 21 BEBOP EXERCISES
*by Steve Rawlins*
This book/CD pack is both a warm-up collection and a manual for bebop phrasing. Its tasty and sophisticated exercises will help you develop your proficiency with jazz interpretation. It concentrates on practice in all twelve keys – moving higher by half-step – to help develop dexterity and range. The companion CD includes all of the exercises in 12 keys.
00315341  Book/CD Pack.................................$17.95

### HAL•LEONARD®
7777 W. BLUEMOUND RD. P.O. BOX 13819 MILWAUKEE, WI 53213

Visit Hal Leonard online at
**www.halleonard.com**

Prices, contents & availability subject to change without notice.

1116